CALIFORNIA
NATIVE AMERICAN TRIBES

IPAI-TIPAI TRIBES
(DIEGUEÑO)

by
Mary Null Boulé

Illustrated by
Daniel Liddell

CONTRA COSTA COUNTY LIBRARY

Merryant Publishing
Vashon, Washington

3 1901 02442 5748

Book Number Five in a series of twenty-six

1

This series is dedicated to Virginia Harding, whose editing expertise and friendship brought this project to fruition.

Library of Congress Catalog Card Number: 92-61897

ISBN: 1-877599-29-8

Copyright © 1992, Merryant Publishing

7615 S.W. 257th St., Vashon, WA 98070.

No part of this book may be reproduced without permission in writing from the publisher.

FOREWORD

Native American people of the United States are often living their lives away from major cities and away from what we call the mainstream of life. It is, then, interesting to learn of the important part these remote tribal members play in our everyday lives.

More than 60% of our foods come from the ancient Native American's diet. Farming methods of today also can be traced back to how tribal women grew crops of corn and grain. Many of our present day ideas of democracy have been taken from tribal governments. Even some 1,500 Native American words are found in our English language today.

Fur traders bought furs from tribal hunters for small amounts of money, sold them to Europeans and Asians for a great deal of money, and became rich. Using their money to buy land and to build office buildings, some traders started business corporations which are now the base of our country's economy.

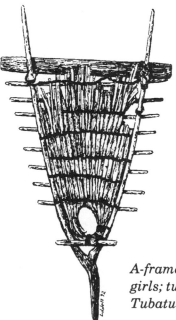

There has never been enough credit given to these early Americans who took such good care of our country when it was still in their care. The time has come to realize tribal contributions to our society today and to give Native Americans not only the credit, but the respect due them.

Mary Boulé

A-frame cradle for girls; tule matting. Tubatulabal tribe.

3

GENERAL INFORMATION

Out of Asia, many thousands of years ago, came Wanderers. Some historians think they were the first people to set foot on our western hemisphere. These Wanderers had walked, step by step, onto our part of the earth while hunting and gathering food. They probably never even knew they had moved from one continent to another as they made their way across a land bridge, a narrow strip of land between Siberia and what is now Russia, and the state of Alaska.

Historians do not know exactly how long ago the Wanderers might have crossed the land bridge. Some of them say 35,000 years ago. What historians do know is that these people slowly moved down onto land that we now call the United States of America. Today it would be very hard to follow their footsteps, for the land bridge has been covered with sea water since the thawing of the ice age.

Those Wanderers who made their way to California were very lucky, indeed. California was a land with good weather most of the year and was filled with plenty of plant and animal foods for them to eat.

The Wanderers who became California's Native Americans did not organize into large tribes like the rest of the North American tribes. Instead, they divided into groups, or tribelets, sometimes having as many as 250 people. A tribelet could number as few as three, to as many as thirty villages located close to each other. Some tribelets had only one chief, a leader who lived in the largest village. Many tribes had a chief for each village. Some leaders had no real power but were thought to be wise. Tribal members always listened with respect to what their chief had to say.

From 20 to 100 people could be living in one village, which usually had several houses. In most cases, these groups of people were related to each other. From five to ten people of one family lived in one house. For instance, a mother, a father, two or three children, a grandmother, or aunt or daughter-in-law might live together.

Village members together would own the land important to them for their well-being. Their land might include oak trees with precious acorns, streams and rivers, and plants which were good to eat. Streams and rivers were especially important to a tribe's quality of life. Water drew animals to it; that meant more food for the tribe to eat. Fish were a good source of food, and traveling by boat was often easier than walking long distances. Water was needed in every part of tribal life.

Village and tribelet land was carefully guarded. Each group knew exactly where the boundaries of its land were found. Boundaries were known by landmarks such as mountains or rivers, or they might also be marked by poles planted in the ground. Some boundary lines were marked by rocks, or by objects placed there by tribal members. The size of a territory had to be large enough to supply food to every person living there.

The California tribes spoke many languages. Sometimes villages close together even had a problem understanding one another. This meant that each group had to be sure of the boundaries of other tribes around them when gathering food. It would not be wise to go against the boundaries and the customs of neighbors. The Native Americans found if they respected the boundaries of their neighbors, not so many wars had to be fought. California tribes, in spite of all their differences, were not as warlike as other tribes in our country.

Not only did the California tribes speak different languages, but their members also differed in size. Some tribes were very tall, almost six feet tall. The shortest people came from the Yuki tribe which had territory in what is now Mendocino County. They measured only about 5'2" tall. All Native Americans, regardless of size, had strong, straight black hair and dark brown eyes.

TRADE

Trading between tribes was an important part of life. Inland tribes had large animal hides that coastal tribes wanted. By trading the hides to coastal groups, inland tribes would receive fish and shells, which they in turn wanted. Coastal tribes also wanted minerals and rocks mined in the mountains by inland tribes. Obsidian rock from the northern mountains was especially wanted for arrowheads. There were, as well, several minerals, mined in the inland mountains, which could be made into the colorful body paints needed for religious ceremonies.

Southern tribes particularly wanted steatite from the Gabrielino tribe. Steatite, or soapstone, was a special metal which allowed heat to spread evenly through it. This made it a good choice to be used for cooking pots and flat frying pans. It could be carved into bowls because of its softness and could be decorated by carving designs into it. Steatite came from Catalina Island in the Coastal Gabrielino territory. Gabrielinos found steatite to be a fine trading item to offer for the acorns, deerskins, or obsidian stone they needed.

When people had no items to trade but needed something, they used small strings of shells for money. The small dentalium shells, which came from the far distant Northwest coast, had great value. Strings of dentalia usually served as money in the Northern California tribes, although some dentalia was used in the Central California tribes.

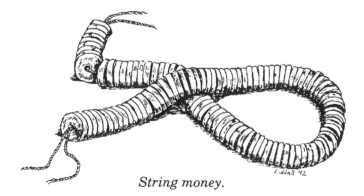

String money.

In southern California clam shells were broken and holes were bored through the center of each piece. Then the pieces were rounded and polished with sandstone and strung into strings for money. These were not thought to be as valuable as dentalia.

Strings of shell money were measured by tattoo marks on the trader's lower arm or hand.

Here is a sample of shell value:

A house, three strings
A fishing place, one to three strings
Land with acorn-bearing oak trees, one to five strings

A great deal of rock and stone was traded among the tribes for making tools. Arrows had to have sharp-edged stone for tips. The best stone for arrow tips was obsidian (volcanic glass) because, when hit properly, it broke off into flakes with very sharp edges. California tribes considered obsidian to be the most valuable rock for trading.

Some tribes had craftsmen who made knives with wooden handles and obsidian blades. Often the handles were decorated with carvings. Such knives were good for trading purposes. Stone mortars and pestles, used by the women for grinding grains into flour, were good trading items.

BASKETS & POTTERY

California tribal women made beautiful baskets. The Pomo and Chumash baskets, what few are left, show us that the women of those tribes might have been some of the finest basketmakers in the world. Baskets were used for gathering and storing food, for carrying babies, and even for hauling water. In emergencies, such as flooding waters, sometimes children, women, and tribal belongings crossed the swollen rivers and streams in huge, woven baskets! Baskets were so tightly woven that not a drop of water could leak from them.

Baskets also made fine cooking pots. Very hot rocks were taken from a fire and tossed around inside baskets with a looped tree branch until food in the basket was cooked.

Most baskets were made to do a certain job, but some baskets were designed for their beauty alone and were excellent for trading. Older women of a tribe would teach young girls how to weave baskets.

Pottery was not used by many California tribes. What little there was seems to have been made by those tribes living near to the Navaho and Mohave tribes of Arizona, and it shows their style. For example, pottery of the California tribes did not have much decoration and was usually a dull red color. Designs were few and always in yellow.

Ohlone hunter wearing deerskin camouflage.

Long thin coils of clay were laid one on top the other. Then the coils were smoothed between a wooden paddle and a small stone to shape the bowl. Pottery from California Native Americans has been described as light weight and brittle (easily broken), probably because of the kind of clay soil found in California.

HUNTING & FISHING

Tribal men spent much of their time making hunting and fishing tools. Bows and arrows were built with great care, to make them shoot as accurately as possible. Carelessly made hunting weapons caused fewer animals to be killed and people then had less food to eat.

Bows made by men of Southern California tribes were made long and narrow. In the northern part of the state bows were a little shorter, thinner, and wider than those of their northern neighbors. Size and thickness of bows depended on the size trees growing in a tribe's territory. The strongest bows were wrapped with sinew, the name given to animal tendons. Sinew is strong and elastic like a rubber band.

Arrows were made in many sizes and shapes, depending on their use. For hunting larger animals, a two-piece arrow was used. The front piece of the arrow shaft was made so that it would remain in the animal, even if the back part was removed or broken off. The arrowhead, or point, was wrapped to the front piece of the shaft. This kind of arrow was also used in wars.

Young boys used a simple wooden arrow with the end sharpened to a point. With this they could hunt small animals like birds and rabbits. The older men of the tribe taught boys how to make their own arrows, how to aim properly, and how to repair broken weapons.

Tribal men spent many hours making and mending fishing nets. The string used in making nets often came from the fibers of plants. These fibers were twisted to make them strong and tough, then knotted into netting. Fences, or weirs, that had one small opening for fish, were built across streams. As the fish swam through the opening they would be caught in netting or harpooned by a waiting fisherman.

Hooks, if used at all, were cut from shells. Mostly hooks could be found when the men fished in large lakes or when catching trout in high mountain areas. Hooks were attached to heavy plant fiber string.

Dip nets, made of netting attached to branches that were bent into a circle, were used to catch fish swimming near shore. Dip nets had long handles so the fishermen could reach deep into the water.

Sometimes a mild poison was placed on the surface of shallow water. This confused the fish and caused them to float to the surface of the water, where they could be scooped up by a waiting fisherman. Not enough poison was used to make humans ill.

Not all fishing was done from the shore. California tribes used two kinds of boats when fishing. Canoes, dug out of one half a log, were useful for river fishing. These were square at each end, round on the bottom, and very heavy. Some of them were well-finished, often even having a carved seat in them.

Today we think of "balsa" as a very lightweight wood, but in Spanish, the word balsa means "raft". That is why Spanish explorers called the Native American canoes, made from tule reeds, "balsa" boats.

Balsa boats were made of bundled tule reeds and were used throughout most of California. They made into safe, light-weight boats for lake and river use. Usually the balsa canoe had a long, tightly tied bundle of tule for the boat bottom and one bundle for each side of the canoe. The front of the canoe was higher than the back. Balsa boats could be steered with a pole or with a paddle, like a raft.

Men did most of the fishing, women were in charge of gathering grasses, seeds, and acorns for food. After the food was collected, it was either eaten right away or made ready for winter storage.

Except for a few southern groups, California tribes had permanent villages where they lived most of the year. They also had food-gathering places they returned to each year to collect acorns, salt, fish, and other foods not found near their villages.

FOOD

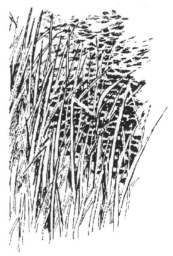

Many different kinds of plant food grew wild in California in the days before white people arrived. Berries and other plant foods grew in the mountains. Forests offered the local tribes everything from pine nuts to animals.

Native Americans found streams full of fish for much of the year. Inland fresh water lakes had large tule reeds growing along their shores. Tule could be eaten as food when plants were young and tender. More important, however, tule was used in making fabric for clothes and for building boats and houses. Tule was probably the most useful plant the California Native Americans found growing wild in their land.

Like all deserts, the one in southern California had little water or fish, but small animals and cactus plants made good food for the local tribes. They moved from place to place harvesting whatever was ripe. Tribal members always knew when and where to find the best food in their territory.

Acorns were the main source of food for all California tribes. Acorn flour was as important to the California Native Americans as wheat is to us today. Five types of California oak trees produced acorns that could be eaten. Those from black oak and tanbark oak seem to have been the favorite kinds.

Since some acorns tasted better than others, the tastiest ones were collected first. If harvest of the favorite acorn was poor some years, then less tasty acorns had to be eaten all winter long.

So important were acorns to California Indians that most tribes built their entire year around them. Acorn harvest marked the beginning of their calendar year. Winter was counted as so many months after acorn harvest, and summer was counted by the number of months before the next acorn harvest.

Acorn harvest ceremonies usually were the biggest events of the year. Most celebrations took place in mid-October and included dancing, feasts, games of chance, and reunions with relatives. Harvest festivals lasted for many days. They were a time of joy for everyone.

The annual acorn gathering lasted two to three weeks. Young boys climbed the oak trees to shake branches; some men used long poles to knock acorns to the ground. Women loaded the nuts into large cone-shaped burden baskets and carried them to a central place where they were put in the sun to dry.

Once the acorns were dried, the women carried them back to the tribe's permanent villages. There they lined special basket-like storage granaries with strong herbs to keep insects away, then stored the acorns inside. Granaries were placed on stilts to keep animals from getting into them and were kept beside tribal houses.

Preparing acorns for each meal was also the women's job. Shells were peeled by hitting the acorns with a stone hammer on an anvil (flat) stone. Meat from the nut was then laid on a stone mortar. A mortar was usually a large stone with a slight dip on its surface. Sometimes the mortar had a bottomless basket, called a hopper, glued to its top. This kept the acorn meat from sliding off the mortar as it was beaten. The meat was then pounded with a long stone pestle. Acorn flour was scraped away from the hopper's sides with a soaproot fiber brush during this process.

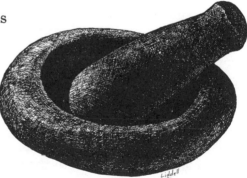

From there the flour was put into an open-worked basket and sifted. A fine flour came through the bottom of the basket, while the larger pieces were put back in the mortar for more pounding.

The most important process came after the acorn flour was sifted. Acorn flour has a very bitter-tasting tannin in it. This bitter taste was removed by a method called leaching. Many tribes leached the flour by first scooping out a hollow in sand near water. The hollow was lined with leaves to keep the flour from washing away. A great deal of hot water was poured through the flour to wash out (leach) the bitterness. Sometimes the flour was put into a basket for the leaching process, instead of using sand and leaves.

Finally the acorn flour was ready to be cooked. To make mush, heated stones were placed in the basket with the flour. A looped tree branch or two long sticks were used to toss the hot rocks around so the basket would not burn. When the mush had boiled, it could be eaten. If the flour and water mixture was baked in an earthen oven, it became a kind of bread. Early explorers wrote that it was very tasty.

Historians have estimated that one family would eat from 1500 to 2000 pounds of acorn flour a year. One reason California native Americans did not have to plant seeds and raise crops was because there were so many acorns for them to harvest each year.

Whether they ate fish or shellfish or plant food or animal meat, nature supplied more than enough food for the Native Americans who lived in California long ago. Many believed their good fortune in having fine weather and plenty to eat came from being good to their gods.

RELIGION

Tribal members had strong beliefs in the power of spirits or gods around them. Each tribe was different, but all felt the importance of never making a spirit angry with them. For that reason a celebration to thank the spirit-gods for treating them well, took place before each food gathering and before each hunting trip, and after each food harvest.

Usually spiritual powers were thought to belong to birds or animals. Most California tribespeople felt bears were very wicked and should not be eaten. But Coyote seems to have been a kind leader who helped them if they were in trouble, even though he seems to have been a bit naughty at times. Eagle was thought to be very powerful and good to native Americans. In some tribes, Eagle was almost as powerful as Sun.

Tribes placed importance on different gods, according to the tribe's needs. Rain gods were the most important spirits to desert tribes. Weather gods, who might bring less rain or warmer temperatures, were important to northern tribes. A great many groups felt there were gods for each of the winds: North, South, East and West. The four directions were usually included in their ceremonial dances and were used as part of the decorations on baskets, pots, and even tools.

Animals were not only worshipped and believed to be spirit-gods, like Deer or Antelope, but tribal members felt there was a personal animal guardian for each one of them. If a tribal member had a deer as guardian, then that person could never kill a deer or eat deer meat.

California Native Americans believed in life after death. This made them very respectful of death and very fearful of angering a dead person. Once someone died, the name of the dead person could never again be said aloud. Since it was easy to accidentally say a name aloud, the name was usually given to a new baby. Then the dead person would not become angry.

Shamans were thought to be the keepers of religious beliefs and to have the ability to talk directly to spirit-gods. It was the job of a village shaman to cure sick people, and to speak to the gods about the needs of the people. Some tribes had several kinds of shamans in one village. One shaman did curing, one scared off evil spirits, while another took care of hunters.

Not all shamans were nice, so people greatly feared their power. However, if shamans had no luck curing sick people or did not bring good luck in hunting, the people could kill them. Most shamans were men, but in a few tribes, women were doctors.

Most California tribal myths have been lost to history because

Religious feather charm.

they were spoken and never written down. The legends were told and retold on winter nights around the home fires. Sadly, these were forgotten after the missionaries brought Christianity to California and moved tribal members into the missions.

A few stories still remain, however. It is thought by historians that northwest California tribes were the only ones not to have a myth on how they were created. They did not feel that the world was made and prepared for human beings. Instead, their few remaining stories usually tell of mountain peaks or rivers in their own territory.

The central California tribes had creation stories of a great flood where there was only water on earth. They tell of how man was made from a bit of mud that a turtle brought up from the bottom of the water.

Many southwest tribes believed there was a time of no sky or water. They told of two clouds appearing which finally became Sky and Earth.

Throughout California, however, all tribes had myths that told of Eagle as the leader, Coyote as chief assistant, and of less powerful spirits like Falcon or Hawk.

Costumes for religious ceremonies often imitated these animals they worshipped or feared. Much time was spent in making the dance costumes as beautiful as possible. Red woodpecker feathers were so brilliant a color they were used to decorate religious headdresses, necklaces, or belts. Deerskin clothing was fringed so shell beads could be attached to each thin strip of leather.

Eagle feathers were felt to be the most sacred of religious objects. Sometimes they were made into whole robes. Usually, though, the feathers were used just for decorations. All these costumes were valuable to the people of each tribe. The village chief was in charge of taking care of the costumes, and there was terrible punishment for stealing them. Clothing worn everyday was not fancy like costuming for rituals.

CLOTHING

Central and southern California's fine weather made regular clothes not really very important to the Native Americans. The children and men went naked most of the year, but most women wore a short apron-like skirt. These skirts were usually made in two pieces, front and back aprons, with fringes cut into the bottom edges. Often the skirt was made from the inner bark of trees, shredded and gathered on a cord. Sometimes the skirt was made from tule or grass.

Willow bark skirt.

In northern California and in rainy or windy weather elsewhere in the state, animal-skin blankets were worn by both men and women. They were used like a cape and wrapped around the body. Sometimes the cape was put over one shoulder and under the other arm, then tied in front. All kinds of skins were used; deer, otter, wildcat, but sea-otter fur was thought to be the best. If the skin was from a small animal, it was cut into strips and woven together into a fabric. At night the cape became a blanket to keep the person warm.

Because of the rainy weather in northern California, the women wore basket caps all the time. Women of the central and south tribes wore caps only when carrying heavy

17

loads, where the forehead had to be used as support. Then a cap helped keep too much weight from being placed on the forehead.

Most California people went barefoot in their villages. For journeys into rough land, going to war, wood gathering, or in colder weather, the tribesmen in central and northwest California wore a one-piece soft shoe with no extra sole, which went high up on the leg.

Southern California tribespeople, however, wore sandals most of the time, wearing high, soled moccasins only when they traveled long distances or into the mountains. Leggings of skin were worn in snow, and moccasins were sometimes lined with grass for more comfort and warmth.

VILLAGE LIFE

Houses of the California tribes were made of materials found in their area. Usually they were round with domed roofs. Except for a few tribes, a house floor was dug into the earth a few feet. This was wise, for it made the home warmer in winter and cooler in summer. It also meant that less material was needed to make house walls.

Framework for the walls was made from bendable branches tied to support poles. Some frames of the houses were covered with earth and grass. Others were covered with large slabs of redwood or pine bark. Central California villagers made large woven mats of tule reed to cover the tops and sides of houses. In the warmer southern area, brush and smaller pieces of bark were used for house walls.

Most California Native American villages had a building called a sweathouse, where the men could be found when they were not hunting, fishing or traveling. It was a very important place for the men, who used it rather like a clubhouse. They could sweat and then scrape themselves clean with curved ribs of deer. The sweathouse was smaller than a family house. Normally it had a center pole framework with a firepit on the ground next to the pole. When the fire was lit, some smoke was allowed to escape through a hole at the top of the roof; however, most was trapped inside the building. Smoke and heat were the main reasons for having a sweathouse. Both were believed to be a way to purify tribal members' bodies. Sweathouse walls were mainly hard-packed earth. The heat produced was not a steam heat but came from a wood-fed fire.

Sweathouse.

In the center of most villages was a large house that often had no walls, just a roof held up with poles. It was here that religious dances and rituals were held, or visitors were entertained.

Dances were enjoyed and were performed with great skill. Music, usually only rhythm instruments, accompanied the dances. For some reason California Native Americans did not use drums to create rhythms for their dances. Three different kinds of rattles were used by California tribes.

One type, split-clap sticks, created rhythm for dancing. These were usually a length of cane (a hollow stick) split in half lengthwise for about two-thirds of its length. The part still uncut was tightly wound with cord so it would not split all the way. The stick was held at the tied end in one hand and hit against the palm of the other hand to make its sound.

A pebble-filled moth cocoon made rhythm for shaman duties. These could range from calling on spirits to cure illnesses, to performing dances to bring rain. Probably the best sounds to beat rhythm for songs and dances came from bundles of deer hooves tied together on a stick. These rattles have a hollow, warm sound.

The only really "musical" instrument found in California was a flute made of reed that was played by blowing across the edge of one end. Melodies were not played on any of these instruments. Most North American Indians sang their songs rather than playing melodies on music instruments.

Special songs were sung for each event. There were songs for healing sick people, songs for success in hunting, war, or marriage. Women sang acorn-grinding songs and lullabies. Songs were sung in sorrow for the dead and during story-telling times. Group singing, with a leader, was the favorite kind of singing. Most songs were sung by all tribe members, but religious songs had to be sung by a special group. It was important that sacred songs not be changed through the years. If a mistake was made while singing sacred music, the singer could be punished, so only specially trained singers would sing ritual songs.

All songs were very short, some of them only 20 to 30 seconds long. They were made longer by repeating the melodies over and over, or by connecting several songs together. Songs usually told no story, just repeated words or phrases or syllables in patterns.

Song melodies used only one or two notes and harmony was never added. Perhaps that is why mission Indians, at those missions with musician priests, especially loved to sing harmony in the church choirs.

Songs and dances were good methods of passing rich tribal traditions on to the children. It was important to tribal adults that their children understand and love the tribe's heritage.

Children were truly wanted by parents in most tribes and new parents carefully watched their tiny babies day and night, to be sure they stayed warm and dry. Usually a newborn was strapped into a cradle and tied to the mother's

Split-stick clapper, rhythm instrument. Hupa tribe.

back so she could continue to work, yet be near the baby at all times. In some tribes, older children took care of babies of cradle age during the day to give the mother time to do all her work, while grandmothers were often in charge of caring for toddlers.

Children were taught good behavior, traditions, and tribal rules from babyhood, although some tribes were stricter than others. Most of the time parents made their children obey. Young children could be lightly punished, but in many tribes those over six or seven years old were more severely punished if they did not follow the rules.

Just as children do today, Native American youngsters had childhood traditions they followed. For instance, one tribal tradition said that when a baby tooth came out, a child waited until dusk, faced the setting sun and threw the tooth to the west. There is no mention of a generous tooth fairy, however.

Tribal parents were worried that their offspring might not be strong and brave. Some tribes felt one way to make their children stronger was by forcing them to bathe in ice cold water, even in wintertime. Every once in a while, for example, Modoc children were awakened from sleep and taken to a cold lake or stream for a freezing bath.

But if freezing baths at night were hard on young Native Americans, their days were carefree and happy. Children were allowed to play all day, and some tribes felt children did not even have to come to dinner if they didn't want to. In those tribes, children could come to their houses to eat anytime of the day.

The games boys played are not too different from those played today. Swimming, hide and seek among the tule reeds, a form of tetherball with a mud ball tied to a pole, and willow-javelin throwing kept boys busy throughout the day.

Fathers made their sons small bows and arrows, so boys spent much time trying to improve their hunting skills. They practised shooting at frogs or chipmunks. The first animal any boy killed was not touched or eaten by him. Others would carry the kill home to be cooked and eaten by villagers. This tradition taught boys always to share food.

Another hunting tool for boys was a hollowed-out willow branch. This became like a modern day beanshooter, only the Native American boys shot juniper berries instead of beans. Slingshots made good hunting weapons, as well.

Girls and boys shared many games, but girls playing with each other had contests to see who could make a basket the fastest, or they played with dolls made of tule. Together, young boys and girls played a type of ring-around-the-rosie game, climbed mountains, or built mud houses.

As children grew older, the boys followed their fathers and the girls followed their mothers as the adults did their daily work. Children were not trained in the arts of hunting or basketmaking, however, until they became teenagers.

HISTORY

Spanish missionaries, led by Fray Junipero Serra, arrived in California in 1769 to build missions along the coast of California. By 1823, fifty years later, 21 missions had been founded. Almost all of them were very successful, and the Franciscan monks who ran them were proud of how many Native Americans became Christians.

However, all was not as the monks had planned it would be. Native American people had never been around the diseases European white men brought with them. As a result, they had no immunity to such illnesses as measles, small pox, or flu. Too many mission Indians died from white men's diseases.

Historians figure there were 300,000 Native Americans living in California before the missionaries came. The missions show records of 83,000 mission Indians during mission days. By the time the Mexicans took over the missions from the Spanish in 1834, only 20,000 remained alive.

The great California Gold Rush of 1849 was probably another big reason why many of the Native Americans died during that time. White men, staking their claim to tribal lands with gold upon it, thought nothing of killing any California tribesman who tried to keep and protect his territory. Fifty-thousand tribal members died from diseases, bullets, or starvation between the gold Rush Days and 1870. By 1910, only 17,000 California Indians remained.

Although the American government tried to set aside reservations (areas reserved for Native Americans), the land given to the Indians often was not good land. Worse yet, some of the land sacred to tribes, such as burial grounds, was taken over by white people and never given back.

Sadly, mission Indians, when they became Christians, forgot the proud heritage and beliefs they had followed for thousands of years. Many wonderful myths and songs they had passed from one generation to the next, on winter nights so long ago, have been lost forever.

Today some 100,000 people can claim California Native American ancestors, but few pure-blooded tribespeople remain. Our link with the Wanderers, who came from Asia so long ago, has been forever broken.

The bullroarer made a deep, loud sound when whirled above the player's head. Tipai tribe.

Villages were usually built beside a lake, stream, or river. Balsa canoes are on the shore. Tule reeds grow along the edge of the water and are drying on poles on the right side of the picture.

Women preparing food in baskets, sit on tule mats. Tule mats are being tied to the willow pole framework of a house being built by one of the men.

IPAI-TIPAI TRIBES
(DIEGUEÑO)

Tipai (Tee pay) and Ipai (Ee pay) were the words used by these two tribes to describe themselves, the land where they lived, and the plant life that grew in their territory. So the meaning in our language might be "people of white sage and eagle".

The name Diegueño was given to them in later years because most members of these two tribes became mission Indians at Mission San Diego in the late 1700s. Mission San Diego was the first of twenty-one missions founded in California by Spain.

For many years the Spanish word Diegueño was used as the name for any group of Native Americans living in Mission San Diego territory, whether the groups had been mission Indians or not. Since the 1950s, however, the Tipai-Ipai names are used by anthropologists (men and women who study how ancient people lived) as a way to describe the language these two groups spoke.

The Tipai and Ipai groups not only spoke the same language, but were alike in many other ways. Both tribes wandered from place to place looking for food and did not even have names for each person, just a family (last) name. Both tribes moved, seasonally, from one food area to another.

Of all the mission tribes in California, the Diegueños were the most stubborn. They violently fought against being a part of mission life. To become mission Indians meant giving up their freedom to wander. Twice within the first six years of Mission San Diego's founding there were deaths. One of those who died was a mission priest, the only priest ever killed by Native Americans during mission years.

THE LAND

Tipai tribelets were found south of today's San Diego, clear into the northern part of Baja California and east to almost the Arizona border. Ipai villages went from San Diego north along the coast to Pala and east to the Salton Sea.

Diegueño land went from sea-level on the coast to 6,500-feet-high mountain peaks and then down below sea-level in the Colorado desert. Many different climates could be found in that territory due to the changes in altitudes. Probably one of the reasons the early tribes moved around so much was because of the different kinds of climates. They traveled up and down mountains and valleys looking for food. Where they wandered depended on the food and the temperature.

Piñon pine trees grew on the lower mountain slopes. Higher up on the mountains, yellow pine and open forests were found. Along the Pacific Ocean coast were beach and marsh plants, then grasslands.

Until about 500 years ago, the Tipais lived around or near Lake Cahuilla, a large freshwater lake which was located in what is today the Imperial Valley. Through the centuries, the temperature in the valley kept rising and the lake began to dry up. As it dried up, it became too salty to drink. Those who study the lives of ancient tribes feel the Tipai-Ipai Indians of explorer times had come nearer to the coast because Lake Cahuilla had evaporated.

THE VILLAGE

Villages of the Diegueño tribes were really only campsites because a tribe was never long at any one place. A campsite was chosen for its water, its protection from weather, and for safekeeping from possible enemy attacks. Land used for a home had to be where no other house had been. There was great fear of sickness being caused by the ghosts of those who had lived there earlier.

A summer village was hardly more than trees or a cave with large rocks to keep the wind away. Summer homes in mountain oak groves were often brush huts or lean-to's. There were usually covered storage granaries in the village. Granaries were actually cone-shaped, coiled baskets placed on platforms or hung from poles. Granaries held dried food gathered for winter meals.

Winter villages were down below the mountains in the warmer valleys. Like summer dwellings, they were built in protected spots where the wind and weather could not reach them. The homes were in clusters, but not built too close together for privacy.

Homes were dome-shaped. They were built with a framework of bending poles, tied together in the center, at the top. To form walls, bundles of grass, or thatch, were laid on top of the framework. Bundles of grass, or thatch, were laid on top of the frame to form walls. This thatch was then covered with dirt and grass. The floor was dug into the ground a few inches.

Framework of house –
bundles of grass were
laid over the
framework.

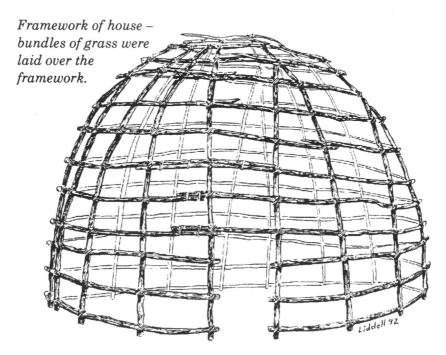

In the desert, palm-leaf thatch walls were put up around four poles. Sometimes sand-covered homes were built near small streams. Tipai tribes living in the mountains might live in large caves in winter, or make homes of slabs of pine wood with bark roofs.

Doorways to the home were built opposite each other and were placed so no wind could blow through them. A separate opening to the east was covered with a grass mat and was put there for religious reasons. Attached to the home was an unroofed area used for summer cooking and for outdoor work.

Ceremonial buildings in the village were owned by everyone. They were usually on a flat piece of ground with brush used as a fence around them. Ceremonial buildings were for dances, rituals and fiestas.

Unlike almost every other California tribe, the sweathouse was not found in their villages. It seems to have not been important to the Diegueños' way of life.

VILLAGE LIFE

Each band or tribelet had a chief and chief's assistant. A chief was usually the eldest son of the chief before him. If the chief had no sons, a brother might take over. Once in a while the widow of a chief would be chosen to lead a clan. Tipais of Imperial Valley did not have clan (village) chiefs, but they did have one chief in charge of all the villages.

A chief was in charge of ceremonies, watched his peoples' behavior, and punished them if needed. The chief also gave advice on marriage, solved family problems, and picked leaders for agave-plant hunts. Assistants to the chief delivered messages and carried out other orders.

A hunt master was chosen to be in charge of village rabbit hunts. He also decided on shaman dances if the chief was gone. Both men and women could become dance leaders and take turns presenting dances. The job of hunt master was passed on to the oldest or best son.

Territory boundary lines of a village were drawn using landmarks such as a mountain or a large rock. If springs of water were in a territory, however, it was for all people to use. Even stored food was shared with strangers and visitors if a promise was given to repay the food later. If plenty of an important plant like agave grew in a tribelet's territory, other families were allowed to harvest the plant. Anyone without a family could not take more than was needed for one person.

Marriages were arranged by parents. A Tipai young man would bring a gift of meat he had killed to a girl's parents to show what a good hunter he was and that he was interested in their daughter. The parents on both sides would exchange presents after a marriage ceremony. This parent-gift exchange went on for as long as the marriage lasted.

Ipai families had a custom of buying brides with fine gifts. A family with many girls could become quite wealthy with such bride presents as food, horses, or rabbit skins.

When a child was born, relatives brought gifts to the new parents. Bedding, food, pots, and baskets were given to celebrate the new baby. It was thought to be an extra blessing if twins were born. Tribe members believed twins to be gifted with supernatural spirits.

The grandparents' job was training children to be good adults. Children's toys were usually small copies of grown-ups' tools so they would learn how to hunt or cook at an early age.

Pottery doll, perhaps for a small child; hollow with a few small pebbles inside.

30

Girls had a celebration when they became teenagers. Their chins were tattooed at the ceremony. It was thought that a tattooed chin would help a girl when she became old. Then, if she ever dribbled food, it would not show. That way, she would still look nice enough when she died so her spirit could travel straight to the afterworld.

Only boys of the Imperial Valley Tipai tribe had a public teenage ceremony. At that time their noses were pierced. Other tribes sometimes pierced boys' noses during a mourning ceremony or at a girl's ceremony.

When a tribal member died, the body, along with the dead person's belongings, was burned with the head of the body facing to the south. Tribespeople believed the afterworld was south of them. Relatives made speeches and wailed during the burning. All-night singing followed, with visitors from friendly nearby villages bringing gifts and joining in the singing.

The name of the dead person was never mentioned again. It was thought bad luck to say aloud the name of a dead person. Those closely related to the dead person cut their hair and blackened their faces with soot.

Women saved the hair they had cut off for an image. Images (life-like dolls) were made and decorated for each person who had died. An image-doll was stuffed to make it look more like the person it represented.

These images were a very important part of the mourning ceremony, which was usually held once a year. Tribal members felt this was a way the spirits of those who had died during the past year could be given one last dance. Songs and wailing went along with the mourning dance.

A mourning ceremony could last from four to eight days. The village saved up extra food all year to feed village people and visitors during the ceremony. Guests would dance with the life-like images and the village members would throw gifts at the guests for dancing. At dawn all the images and costumes were thrown in one big pile and burned.

RELIGION AND BELIEFS

Songs, dances and ground paintings were all based on tribal myths. These myths speak of Earth Mother (the first woman) and Primal Water (first man), who became Sky when he was lifted up by his sons. Diegueños believed these two gods created everything from humans to the universe around them. Foxes were thought to be pets of the gods. Certain animal spirits, like Eagle and Mountain Lion, were honored. Frog was hated and Coyote was not trusted.

Ground paintings were often made at ceremonies for teen-agers. Ground paintings used special color symbols to explain directions. In the paintings, east (white) was paired with west (black). North (red) was paired with south (blue).

Ipai tribelets had more ceremonies than the Tipais did. Ipais had special performances. Magic tricks were performed by shamans and religious dances were presented. In the Fire ceremony, shamans put out fire with their hands and feet.

The Eagle ceremony was celebrated to honor dead chiefs and shamans. A tamed eagle was killed with great sadness in this ritual. Its death was mourned as a human death would be. The body was then cremated and the feathers saved.

Ipai shamans danced the War Dance in which the song became higher and higher in pitch. A raised fist came at each change of pitch.

In the Whirling Dance, Ipais had one performer who painted his body in white stripes. He wore an eagle-feather skirt and a headband of owl feathers. During the dance he would whirl in one spot. Usually rattles made from gourds pottery or turtle shells beat out the rhythm.

Travel always meant social and religious dances, ceremonies and games. When gathering food, tribe members would often stay at Mountain Springs just to have social dances. When piñon nuts were harvested, a Piñon-Bird dance was held. This dance had two lead singers, a man and a woman, and used a gourd rattle for rhythm.

Turtle-shell rattle.
Vegetable fiber netting
holds shell together.

The keepers of spirits and myths were the village shamans. There were almost no women shamans. Most shamans were well trained in many areas, but they were expert in only one or two kinds of rituals. For instances, a shaman might choose to do only such things as curing with herbs, explaining dreams, or finding a place to hunt large animals. Some shamans were thought to be able to predict weather. A few were thought to be "born" shamans who could transform themselves into their guardian animals.

Those with guardian animals of Rattlesnake and Bear were greatly feared. Indeed, some shamans were thought to be evil, and a curing shaman was often called upon to undo the evil of a bad shaman.

FOOD

The desert-like climate in the Tipai territory meant there was rain only in the winter and drought (a long time of no rain) in the summer. In spite of not much water, nature brought forth many kinds of wild plants for food and for making useful items.

Chaparral plants grew in the area west of the desert. Some scrub oak trees, Joshua trees, wild lilac, and elderberries grew there. Farther south were desert plants which stored their own water, such as yucca and maguey plants. From here the land gave way to brush desert and finally true desert. Food of many kinds could be found in most places except for the true desert in the summer.

Tribe members looking for food moved higher as the seasons became warmer. As spring changed to summer, they moved from the low canyons to the higher mountain slopes. Two or three families would come to a campsite at one time to gather ripe food. Preparing the food for storage was done right at the campsite. Food for the winter would be stored when the clans, or village people, went back to the lower land for winter.

Some tribal members left the village to harvest agave in the month of May. These agave cactus plants were dried and stored in foothill caves for winter food. From June through August ripe wild seeds were collected from the lowlands, and wild fruits, such as plums, could be gathered in low mountain areas. The Imperial Valley Tipais gathered mesquite pods in July. Other tribes worked hard in the mountains from September through November to gather and prepare acorns and piñon nuts. Men of the tribes hunted for deer and rabbits to be preserved for winter meals. When snow fell, the people went down to their winter homes.

Acorns from six kinds of oak trees were a major food of all but the Valley Tipai tribe. Valley Tipai people depended on dried mesquite pounded into flour for their main food. Flour ground from sage plants was the second most important plant food for most villages.

The women cooked mush and cakes from dried flour. Stews of meat and wild vegetables were cooked in pots set over a fire. Seeds were cooked by stirring them with hot pieces of granite rock in an olla (pottery jar) set on three stones over a fire. The seeds were then stored in another pottery jar.

Cactus was picked with stick tongs and placed into mesh bags so could be rolled around until the sharp spines fell off. Such cacti as agave, yucca, cholla, and prickly pair were used for food.

Men did most of the work when a village went to gather agave plants. These plants were too large to be harvested by women. Often many family groups, or villages, worked together to cut the agave. The tribes used methods they had learned from Mexican Tipais. The plant was cooked in one large covered pit with each group of people keeping its agave separate from the others. Sap from the plant was stored in small gourd jars and used for blackening mourners' faces. Baked agave was sun-dried, pounded, and then flattened to take home for food in wintertime.

Fresh plants included watercress, two kinds of clover, many kinds of grasses, and yucca roots. Manzanita berries and elderberries were favorites of these tribes and were eaten fresh or dried.

Meat was roasted on coals or in ashes. Some bones were ground up into a flour for making a thin soup. Lizards, some snakes, and insects were also eaten. Sometimes rodents (rabbits or rats) and birds were the only meat hunters found to eat.

The Imperial Valley Tipai women would often plant wild corn, beans, and melons on newly flooded land. They also transplanted wild-onion plants nearer to their villages. It is interesting to know, however, that if the time to harvest food they had gathered for centuries came before they had harvested their planted foods, the planted foods were left to rot in the fields. It was always important to follow the ways of the tribes' ancestors, so the gathering of food they had always eaten was more important than food they had just learned to plant.

HUNTING AND FISHING

Coastal tribes, and those who lived by streams of water, ate much fish. Using bows, nets and hooks, the fishermen climbed into tule boats to catch the fish. Tule boats were made by tying bundles of tule together. Sometimes the foothill tribelets joined the coastal people in getting fish. The mountain tribelets did not like fish so never went fishing.

Wood rats were shot with a bow and arrow or caught in traps. Rabbits were killed with a throwing stick as well as with a bow and arrow. A small type of dog (now extinct) was trained to round up small animals, or to scare them out of their holes in the ground.

Quails could actually be hand-caught when they were cold or wet, or when fires had been built to smoke-blind them. Mockingbirds and roadrunners were caged for pets.

The Diegueño tribes did not have large animals to kill. Nevertheless, they knew a great deal about animal habits and used excellent hunting methods. They had a hunter's set of signal codes, knew stars and their positions in the sky, and had a fine attitude toward animals and people. Hunters also had songs they sang and myths they told and retold.

Men made their own hunting weapons and tools. Grandfathers taught their grandsons the art of hunting. A good hunter tested his grandsons on killing rats before he taught them about rabbits. He taught only the best students about hunting larger animals.

Each boy dreamed of being allowed to go on a hunt led by a hunt master, and it was a most exciting day when a boy killed his first deer. All the meat from a boy's first-killed deer went to villagers and relatives. It was bad luck for a young hunter to eat meat from his first deer.

On an important hunt, older men carried the equipment and supplies so the younger adults would be free to stalk animals and kill them. The older men also carried the meat back to the village.

Young hunters had certain jobs when hunting. Some were trail-sitters and some were trackers who found animals and followed (stalked) them until the animals could be killed. Ground paintings of hunters showed drawings of a constellation (pattern of stars in the sky) in which Mountain Sheep (three stars) are trailed by a hunter (a large star in the eastern sky) with trail-sitters shown by two other stars nearby. Before a hunt, the hunters would try to study their dreams for good or bad signs of their luck in the coming hunt. A hunter usually went without food before a hunt or drank only a thin, watery soup. A hunter was careful to keep away from dead bodies before going hunting.

A hunter never ate any of his first-killed deer each year. Instead, the meat was given to old people at home, and some of it was shared with his fellow hunters. If the hunter owed anyone a debt, that person got part of the deer meat. Meat was also a good trading item.

Throwing stick used for killing small animals. Although curved, it did not return to thrower, as an Australian boomerang does.

TRADING

Diegueño tribes traded more with each other than with unrelated tribes. Coastal Tipais traded salt, dried seafood, dried vegetable greens, and abalone shells for the inland tribes' acorns, agave, mesquite beans, and gourds.

Valley (inland) Tipais traded to get eaglet feathers, yucca fiber for sandal-making, and agave fiber and juncus grasses for stuffing mourning-image frames. Valley Tipais also had to trade to get granite rock for pestles, steatite (soapstone) to use for arrow straighteners, and red-and-black minerals for paint. After the Europeans brought horses to the California territory, it was known that an eagle or its feathers were a good trade for a horse.

Upland tribes manufactured such items as carrying nets, basket caps, and winnowing trays which the Valley Tipais wanted. They also wanted the upland tribe's seed and acorn flour and its prepared agave plants.

BASKETS AND POTTERY

While gathering food, the women also collected grasses for the coiled baskets they made. Flat winnowing baskets were used for removing stalks from the grain. Large baskets held fruit and nuts knocked down from trees. Small hopper baskets with no bottoms were glued to stone mortars. These hoppers were needed to keep the grain from blowing away as it was being ground with a stone pestle.

Pottery was mostly not decorated, but it sometimes had a pattern in reddish-brown colors. Pottery was made by the paddle and anvil method. Coils of clay were piled one atop the other. The bowl or object then was smoothed with a small stone on one side and a paddle on the other.

Pottery jars were used to store and carry water. Pottery bowls and pieces of pottery became cooking pots. Only a few southern California tribes had the right clay soil for making pottery. Sometimes large gourds, like pottery, were used for carrying water.

CLOTHING

Diegueño people wore little, if any, clothing. Men and children never felt they needed clothes, but men sometimes wore a waist cord to carry objects they might use during the day. Men would sometimes wear a coiled basket cap on their heads. Women wore one- or two-piece aprons. On her head a woman wore a round, twined basket cap to protect her forehead from the packstrap holding her carrying net. A carrying net held heavy loads of food, utensils, or clothing and was carried on women's backs.

All southern tribes went barefoot or wore open sandals. Ipai-Tipai sandals were made of fiber from the agave plant. For traveling, these sandals had a padded sole of leaves. Robes of rabbitskin, buckskin, or willow bark were worn in cooler weather and became blankets at night.

Hair hung long with bangs on the forehead, except for boys or those people mourning for a dead relative. Some Imperial Tipais wore long pencil-like coils of hair. Men pulled out face whiskers with their fingers. Women tattooed their chins and decorated their faces every day with red, white, and black designs.

Small children had pierced ears with tiny deer leg bones as earrings. Boys' noses were pierced so that as men, they could hang a small ornament there, or put a stick through the nose.

Special, but not fancy, costumes and ornaments were worn at ceremonies.

HISTORY

In 1779, ten years after the founding of Mission San Diego, there were 1,405 mission Indians living near the mission. Slowly, more members of the Ipai-Tipai tribes became mission workers. In the mid-1850s, there were thought to be 2,500 tribal members.

In 1834 the Mexicans, who had driven Spanish priests from the missions, offered mission buildings and land for sale to anyone who wanted to buy them. Spain had promised to give mission Indians at least

Deer hoof rattle; handle is of vegetable fiber rope; about 11 inches high.

half of the mission land to use for farming. The Mexicans did not keep this promise, and land given to the Diegueño tribes was taken back. Tribal people became slaves to Mexican land owners.

When American settlers arrived to claim land, the United States government formed many reservations for the tribelets. Most reservations were placed where tribe villages already were located. However, in coastal Ipai territory new settlers had begun to build cities. The Ipais had nowhere to go. Many lived in slum areas in San Diego, or camped on hillsides outside of town.

Those tribespeople who had never been mission Indians kept on living more or less as they had before the missionaries came. Tipai-Ipai people have been fortunate enough to keep many of their centuries-old customs. This was possible because when the United States government assigned Native Americans to reservation land, the Diegueños were given parts of their own ancient territory. They have been able to care for their own sacred cemeteries, and some ancient villages are still home to the tribal members.

There are some places in Baja California today where Tipai children are being taught the Tipai language first, before they learn Spanish or English. In the United States, there are fewer Diegueño people every year speaking their native language. While many people still spoke Tipai language at the end of the 1800s, very few speak the language today.

Many of the reservations now have fiestas which bring together different cultures. Native American, Spanish, and Mexican customs are combined into a delightful mixture of religious and nonreligious celebrations enjoyed by everyone. Old and new games and sports are played and barbecued meals are served. It is good that the Ipai-Tipai tribes have kept some of their heritage to use in their lives each day.

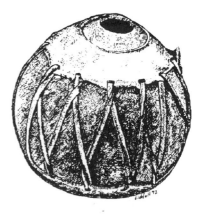

Gourds used to carry water. Leather covers outside of gourd.

OUTLINE
IPAI-TIPAI (DIEGUEÑO)

I. Introduction
   A. Names of tribes
   B. How Ipai and Tipai tribes were alike
   C. Tribes' feelings about mission
II. The land
   A. Territory boundaries
   B. Describe altitudes (highs and lows) of territory
   C. Kinds of climate
III. The village
   A. Winter houses
   B. Summer campsite shelters
   C. Mountain caves
   D. Ceremonial buildings
IV. Village life
   A. Chief
      1. How chosen
      2. No village chiefs
      3. Duties
      4. Chief's assistant
   B. Hunt master
      1. Duties
   C. Village boundary landmarks
      1. How water and food was shared
   D. Tipai marriage
      1. Describe
   E. Ipai marriage
      1. Describe
   F. Birth of children
   G. Training of children

H. Teenage girls' celebration and tattoos

I. Teenage boys' ceremony and nose piercing

J. Death

    1. Customs of mourning and burial

    2. Afterworld beliefs

    3. Image-dance

V. Religion and beliefs

A. Myths

    1. Creating of universe

B. Animal spirits

    1. Fox

    2. Eagle and Mountain Lion

    3. Coyote and Frog disliked

C. Ground paintings

D. Ceremonies of Ipai and Tipai

E. Religious and social dances

F. Shamans

VI. Food

A. Kinds of food and where it was found

B. Preparing of food

    1. Kinds of containers used for cooking

    2. Kinds of cooking

VII. Hunting and fishing

A. Fishing equipment used

    1. Tule boats

B. Hunting equipment used

    1. Tools, trained dogs

    2. Use of smoke

C. No large fish or animals eaten

D. Made own hunting weapons

E. Boys taught methods by grandfathers

F. Older men carried equipment on hunts, carried meat back to village

G. Dreams important to hunt success
VIII. Trading
    A. Most trading among tribal villages
        1. Items traded
    B. Worth of horse
IX. Baskets and pottery
    A. Type of weave used
    B. Kinds of baskets made
    C. Kinds and uses of pottery
X. Clothing
    A. Men
    B. Women
    C. Children
XI. History
    A. Number of tribal members in 1850s
    B. Mexican rule
    C. American rule
        1. Reservations
        2. Diegueño homes off-reservation
    D. Tipai language
    E. Fiestas

GLOSSARY

AWL: a sharp, pointed tool used for making small holes in leather or wood

CEREMONY: a meeting of people to perform formal rituals for a special reason; like an awards ceremony to hand out trophies to those who earned honors

CHERT: rock which can be chipped off, or flaked, into pieces with sharp edges

COILED: a way of weaving baskets which looks like the basket is made of rope coils woven together

DIAMETER: the length of a straight line through the center of a circle

DOWN: soft, fluffy feathers

DROUGHT: a long period of time without water

DWELLING: a building where people live

FLETCHING: attaching feathers to the back end of an arrow to make the arrow travel in a straight line

GILL NET: a flat net hanging vertically in water to catch fish by their heads and gills

GRANARIES: basket-type storehouses for grains and nuts

HERITAGE: something passed down to people from their long-ago relatives

LEACHING: washing away a bitter taste by pouring water through foods like acorn meal

MORTAR: flat surface of wood or stone used for the grinding of grains or herbs with a pestle

PARCHING:	to toast or shrivel with dry heat
PESTLE:	a small stone club used to mash, pound, or grind in a mortar
PINOLE:	flour made from ground corn
INDIAN RESERVATION:	land set aside for Native Americans by the United States government
RITUAL:	a ceremony that is always performed the same way
SEINE NET:	a net which hangs vertically in the water, encircling and trapping fish when it is pulled together
SHAMAN:	tribal religious men or women who use magic to cure illness and speak to spirit-gods
SINEW:	stretchy animal tendons
STEATITE:	a soft stone (soapstone) mined on Catalina Island by the Gabrielino tribe; used for cooking pots and bowls
TABOO:	something a person is forbidden to do
TERRITORY:	land owned by someone or by a group of people
TRADITION:	the handing down of customs, rituals, and belief, by word of mouth or example, from generation to generation
TREE PITCH:	a sticky substance found on evergreen tree bark
TWINING:	a method of weaving baskets by twisting fibers, rather than coiling them around a support fiber

NATIVE AMERICAN WORDS WE KNOW AND USE

PLANTS AND TREES
hickory
pecan
yucca
mesquite
saguaro

ANIMALS
caribou
chipmunk
cougar
jaguar
opossum
moose

STATES
Dakota – friend
Ohio – good river
Minnesota – waters that
    reflect the sky
Oregon – beautiful water
Nebraska – flat water
Arizona
Texas

FOODS
avocado
hominy
maize (corn)
persimmon
tapioca
succotash

GEOGRAPHY
bayou – marshy body of
    water
savannah – grassy plain
pasadena – valley

WEATHER
blizzard
Chinook (warm, dry wind)

FURNITURE
hammock

HOUSE
wigwam
wickiup
tepee
igloo

INVENTIONS
toboggan

BOATS
canoe
kayak

OTHER WORDS
caucus – group meeting
mugwump – loner politician
squaw – woman
papoose – baby

CLOTHING
moccasin
parka
mukluk – slipper
poncho

BIBLIOGRAPHY

Cressman, L. S. *Prehistory of the Far West.* Salt Lake City, Utah: University of Utah Press, 1977.

Heizer, Robert F., volume editor. *Handbook of North American Indians; California, volume 8.* Washington, D.C.: Smithsonian Institute, 1978.

Heizer, Robert F. and Elsasser, Albert B. *The Natural World of the California Indians.* Berkeley and Los Angeles, CA; London, England: University of California Press, 1980.

Heizer, Robert F. and Whipple, M.A.. *The California Indians.* Berkeley and Los Angeles, CA; London, England: University of California Press, 1971.

Heuser, Iva. *California Indians.* PO Box 352, Camino, CA 95709: Sierra Media Systems, 1977.

Macfarlen, Allen and Paulette. *Handbook of American Indian Games.* 31 E. 2nd Street, Mineola, N.Y. 11501: Dover Publications, 1985.

Murphey, Edith Van Allen. *Indian Uses of Native Plants.* 603 W. Perkins Street, Ukiah, CA 95482: Mendocino County Historical Society, © renewal, 1987.

National Geographic Society. *The World of American Indians.* Washington, DC: National Geographic Society reprint, 1989.

Tunis, Edwin. *Indians.* 2231 West 110th Street, Cleveland, OH: The World Publishing Company, 1959.

Weatherford, Jack. *Native Roots.* 201 E. 50th Street, New York, NY 10022: Crown Publishers, 1991.

Credits:
Island Industries, Vashon Island, Washington 98070
Dona McAdam, Mac on the Hill, Seattle, Washington 98109

Acknowledgements:
Richard Buchen, Research Librarian, Braun Library,
Southwest Museum
Special thanks

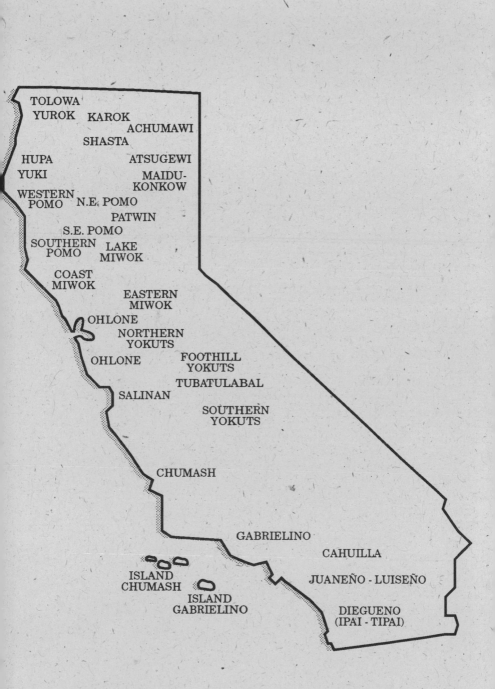

TOLOWA
YUROK   KAROK
              ACHUMAWI
        SHASTA
HUPA   ATSUGEWI
YUKI   MAIDU-
                KONKOW
WESTERN
POMO   N.E. POMO
          PATWIN
      S.E. POMO
SOUTHERN   LAKE
  POMO   MIWOK
    COAST
    MIWOK
          EASTERN
          MIWOK
      OHLONE
        NORTHERN
        YOKUTS
    OHLONE   FOOTHILL
              YOKUTS
            TUBATULABAL
      SALINAN
              SOUTHERN
              YOKUTS

            CHUMASH

                GABRIELINO
                        CAHUILLA
    ISLAND
    CHUMASH   JUANEÑO - LUISEÑO
          ISLAND
          GABRIELINO
                    DIEGUENO
                    (IPAI - TIPAI)

Map Art: Dona McAdam

At last, a detailed book on the Ipai-Tipai Tribe written just for students

Mary Null Boulé taught in the California public school system for twenty-five years. Her teaching years made her aware of the acute need for well-researched regional social studies books for elementary school students. This series on the California Native American tribes fills a long-standing need in California education. Ms. Boulé is also author and publisher of *The Missions: California's Heritage*. She is married and the mother of five grown children.

Illustrator Daniel Liddell has been creating artistic replicas of Native American artifacts for several years, and his paintings reflect his own Native American heritage. His paternal grandmother was full-blood Chickasaw.

ISBN: 877599-29-8